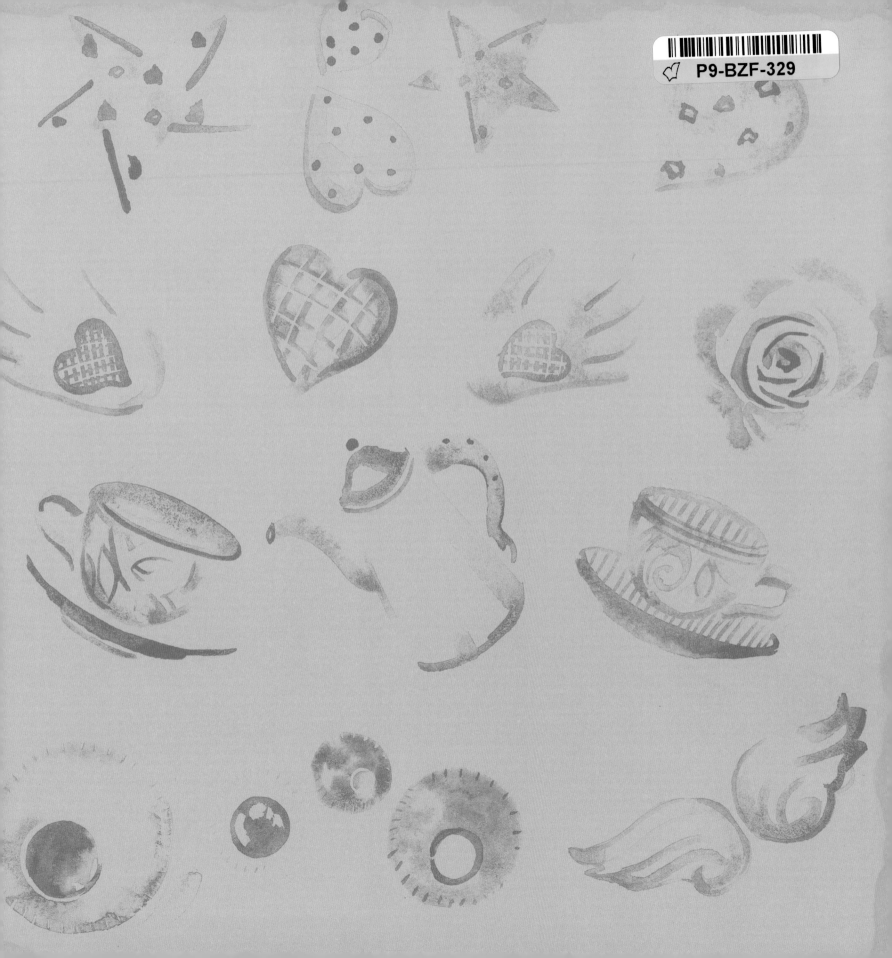

NEW CRAFTS

APPLIQUÉ

NEW CRAFTS
APPLIQUÉ
PETRA BOASE

PHOTOGRAPHY BY POLLY WREFORD

LORENZ BOOKS
NEW YORK • LONDON • SYDNEY • BATH

This edition published in 1997 by
Lorenz Books, 27 West 20th Street,
New York, New York 10011

Lorenz Books are available for bulk
purchase for sales promotion and for
premium use. For details, write or call
the manager of special sales:
Lorenz books, 27 West 20th Street,
New York, NY 10011
(800) 354-9657

© Anness Publishing Limited 1997

Lorenz Books is an imprint of
Anness Publishing Limited

ISBN 1 85967 530 1

Publisher: Joanna Lorenz
Senior Editor: Lindsay Porter
Designer: Lilian Lindblom
Step Photographer: Mark Wood
Stylist: Leeann Mackenzie
Illustrators: Madeleine David and
Vana Haggerty

Printed and bound in Hong Kong

10 9 8 7 6 5 4 3 2 1

PICTURE CREDITS
The author and publishers would like to thank the following for additional photography: Victoria and Albert Museum, pp. 8 and 9;
Patrick Gorman, p. 10 and Joseph Ortenzi, p. 17

CONTENTS

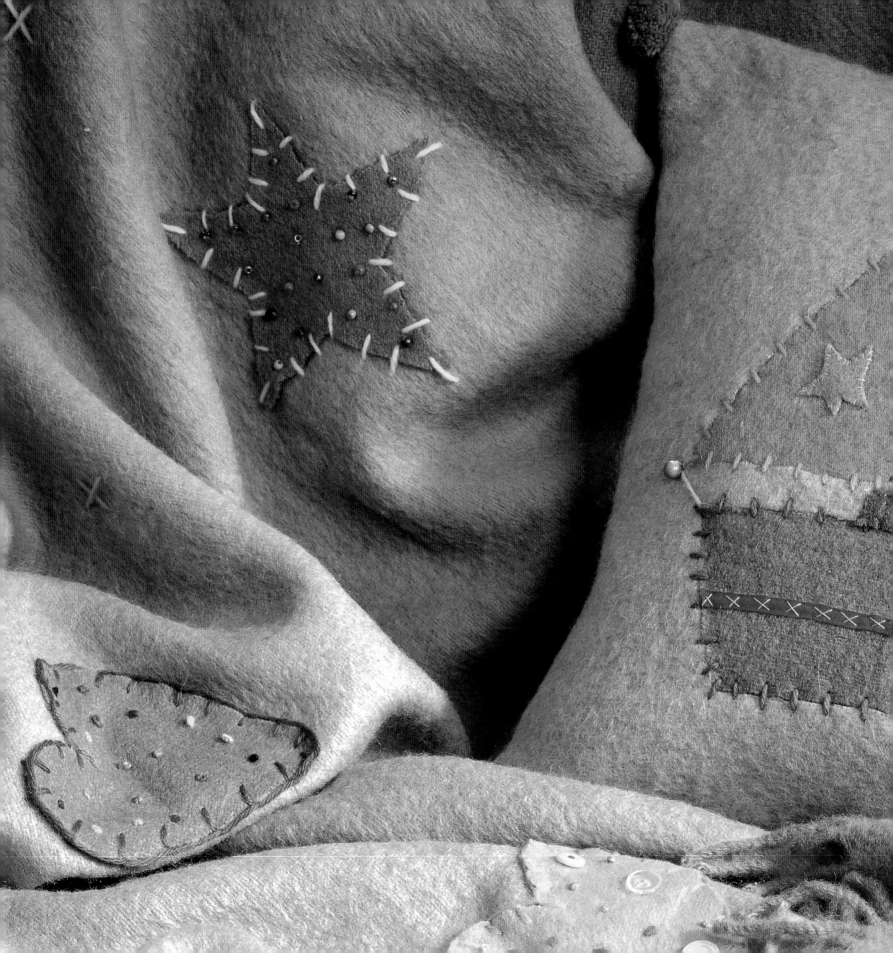

INTRODUCTION

PPLIQUÉ IS A VERSATILE METHOD OF APPLYING AND SECURING PIECES OF FABRIC ONTO A BACKGROUND, THEN ENRICHING WITH DECORATIVE STITCHES. APPLIQUÉ HAS BEEN PRACTICED ALL OVER THE WORLD FOR CENTURIES AND, OVER THAT TIME, MANY DIFFERENT STYLES AND TECHNIQUES HAVE EVOLVED. THERE ARE NO LIMITATIONS TO WHAT IS POSSIBLE WITH APPLIQUÉ; FINISHED PIECES CAN BE BOLD AND COLORFUL, PICTORIAL OR ABSTRACT, AND DESIGNS CAN BE EITHER SIMPLE OR COMPLEX. THE 25 DIVERSE AND EXCITING PROJECTS IN THIS BOOK WHICH USE AN ASSORTMENT OF DISTINCTIVE FABRICS AND DECORATIVE TRIMMINGS AND STITCHES, PROVIDE EXAMPLES OF DIFFERENT METHODS OF APPLIQUÉ YOU CAN USE TO CREATE ITEMS BOTH LOVELY AND FUNCTIONAL.

Left: Simple shapes in ice-cream colors are used to great effect in these appliqué designs, demonstrating that strikingly contemporary pieces can be created from an age-old technique.

HISTORY OF APPLIQUÉ

APPLIQUÉ HAS BEEN PRACTICED FOR CENTURIES BY MOST CULTURES THROUGHOUT THE WORLD. ITS ORIGINS WERE INITIALLY PRACTICAL: SCRAPS OF CLOTH COULD BE REUSED BY SEWING THEM TO BACKGROUND FABRICS, THUS PROLONGING THE LIFE OF CLOTHING AND MATERIALS THAT MAY HAVE BEEN SCARCE. IT IS INTERESTING TO TRACE HOW THESE CONCERNS INSPIRED A MEANS OF CREATIVE EXPRESSION; THE FABRICS COULD BE CUT INTO ATTRACTIVE SHAPES AND EMBELLISHED WITH STITCHING. AS DIFFERENT TECHNIQUES DEVELOPED INDEPENDENTLY THROUGHOUT THE WORLD, VARYING STYLES EMERGED.

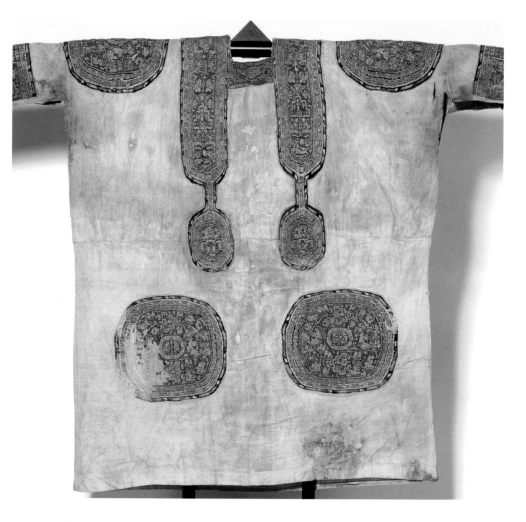

Although appliqué developed very simply as a method of repairing worn items of clothing, examples have been found dating back as far as 980 BC when animal hides were used by the ancient Egyptians to embellish funeral tents.

During the Middle Ages, appliqué became a very fashionable and functional method of working for needleworkers; because of its relatively low cost, it became a strong substitute for the more costly and time-consuming solid embroidery. Fabrics were applied to items as diverse as household furnishings, heraldic flags and costumes. Appliqué was especially popular on ecclesiastical robes and altar frontals. In these instances, linen shapes were cut out and applied to a velvet or silk background with an edging of cord or silk strands. The appliquéd shapes would then be embellished with rich gold stitching.

During the Renaissance, appliqué became a lavish form of embellishment on furnishings and hangings throughout the palaces and castles of the upper classes and royalty. As well as being exquisitely executed and beautifully decorated, many of the appliquéd hangings were hung and draped around the home for warmth, especially in doorways and around four-poster beds to shut out drafts. In peasant cultures, the appliqué tradition was equally strong; precious remnants of more costly fabrics such as silk would be cut into shapes and appliquéd onto damaged parts of clothing or applied to domestic , articles. This grew from economic necessits

ity, but it also created many sophisticated results. Thus appliqué became strongly associated with folk art, and evidence of the technique appears in most cultures throughout the world. In Hungary, leather appliqué became very popular among peasant societies and was very much a status symbol because of the expense involved.

Above: Appliqué examples have been found dating back centuries and practical motives, such as repairing worn clothing, soon gave way to decorative effects. This leather tunic dates from 6–7th century AD. The appliqué inserts are made of fine woven tapestry.

Throughout the United States, appliqué developed independently through quilt designs. Patterns were handed down from generation to generation and were often based on natural imagery such as birds, baskets, fruit, bouquets of flowers and garlands. Economy made the quilt popular throughout America as each scrap of fabric left over from cutting clothing was saved, and quilts were an essential part of the home for practical reasons because of the austere winters. Some quilts had so much work put into them that they were kept for privileged guests or for display in the home.

Many of the techniques that inspire contemporary work draw on the intricate and unusual methods practiced throughout Southeast Asia and India. In India, appliqué was commonly used to make religious hangings for festivals and ceremonies. The fabrics chosen would often depend on the importance of the event. The images portrayed throughout the designs were often drawn from mythology and were very spiritually symbolic. In Southeast Asia, intricate maze patterns were created using a cutwork method. The designs were highly intricate and were used in the decoration of clothing and hangings. In many tribes, the skill is still a very central part of women's work. The 20th century brought exciting and innovative design movements. Today, appliqué is rich and varied in style and is used for many different applications. Many of the methods used are drawn from traditional techniques practiced throughout history all over the world. Machine-stitching has become a very popular method of applying and embellishing appliqué shapes, and there are now many forms of fabric bondings and adhesives on the market to aid faster methods of appliqué. Appliqué is often seen as the fabric equivalent to

paper collage and should be executed in a similarly spontaneous way. Be as expressive as you want with your choice of fabrics and embellishments, and don't let complicated techniques restrict the flow and imagination of your designs.

Above: A beautiful example of a decorative panel dating from 19th-century Persia. Brightly coloured woolen cloth pieces were applied to a main background fabric and embellished with decorative embroidery stitches, including chain stitches. This exquisite example of the needleworker's art combines many of the most appealing aspects of appliqué.

GALLERY

DESIGNERS TODAY ARE USING APPLIQUÉ TO CREATE A WONDERFUL VARIETY AND RANGE OF OBJECTS AND EFFECTS. THE PIECES ON THE FOLLOWING PAGES START WITH THE SAME BASIC TECHNIQUE, BUT THE RESULTS ARE AS DIVERSE AS THEIR CREATORS. THE FOLLOWING EXAMPLES USE MATERIALS FROM PAPER TO PLASTIC AND ALL MANNER OF NATURAL FABRICS. LET THEM BE A STARTING POINT FOR YOUR OWN PERSONAL CREATIONS.

Right: TIC-TAC-TOE
This embroidered wall hanging is made in nine sections using a combination of hand- and machine-stitching to appliqué silk, cotton, chiffon and velvet onto a background fabric.
CHARLOTTE HODGE

Left: DOT LAMPSHADE
A fabric-covered shade
is embellished with buttons
and bright circles of
color using the cutwork
technique. The appliqué
shapes are sewn behind the
background fabric, which
is then cut away to reveal
the new colors beneath.
HELEN RAWLINSON

Above: SHOWER
CURTAIN
Brightly colored vinyl
fabric and bold designs are
used to great effect in this
eye-catching design.
ANNE DELAUNEY

Far right and right: PAPER
APPLIQUÉ HANGING
AND DETAIL
The ingenious combina-
tion of materials and sub-
tle tones makes this piece
very striking. Handmade
paper squares are stitched
onto a background fabric.
Small squares of hand-
painted muslin form the
central motif.
CHRISTINE SMITH

Left: WALL HANGING
The artist uses
photographic images
transferred onto fabric,
which are then appliquéd
onto a background fabric.
NATASHA KERR

Opposite: HAT AND
PURSE
These pieces were made
by first hand-knitting the
basic shapes and felting
them by washing in warm
soapy water. When dry,
the elements are sewn
together, with additional
felted knitting and com-
mercial felt appliquéd on
top. The resulting richly
textured fabric is
wonderfully tactile.
TERESA SEARLE

Right: SHADOW-
APPLIQUÉ VEST
Natural linen forms the
basis of this vest, made
special by the appliqué
designs on the pockets.
The pattern pieces were
cut from scraps of colored
silk, machine-stitched in
place, then covered with a
layer of organza.
LOUISE BROWNLOW

Right: CHILD'S
CARDIGAN
Felt patchwork pieces in
harlequin colors are
decorated with simple felt
shapes held in place with
contrasting-colored
threads. Blanket stitch
finishes off the cuffs
and hems.
KATIE MAWSON

Above: WALL HANGING
Architectural shapes are
used in an almost abstract
manner in this appliquéd
and machine-embroidered
hanging.
CHARLOTTE HODGE

Left: HAT AND SCARF
This matching hat and scarf set for a child is a perfect example of how simple yet strong embellishments can transform an object. Rich textures, bold colors and stitches all combine to make an appealing and original design.
KATIE MAWSON

Above: TOILETRY BAG
The perfect accessory for the designer's shower curtain, the basic shape was made using a patchwork technique, then decorated with quirky designs held in place with a running stitch.
ANNE DELAUNEY

MATERIALS

YOUR OWN CHOICE OF FABRICS, TRIMMINGS AND EMBELLISHMENTS IS WHAT MAKES A PIECE OF APPLIQUÉ WORK PERSONAL AND UNIQUE. SELECT FABRICS CAREFULLY AND COLLECT AS MANY AS POSSIBLE TO CHOOSE FROM. LOOK FOR REMNANTS AT REDUCED PRICES AND NEVER THROW LEFTOVER SCRAPS OF FABRIC AWAY—YOU WILL FIND A USE FOR THEM ONE DAY. BELOW ARE SOME OTHER MATERIALS THAT MAY BE USEFUL FOR APPLIQUÉ.

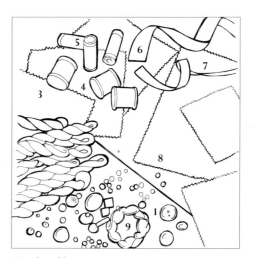

Beads and buttons These are both available in a wide range of colors, materials, sizes and shapes. Use buttons for decoration as well as fastening, and to fasten quilts. Do not use buttons or beads on children's projects.

Craft adhesive spray This is a spray-on glue that should be used sparingly and in a well-ventilated area. It is useful for attaching fabric to cardboard.

Double-sided tape This is used to stick fabric onto cardboard or paper.

Embroidery floss This is available in many different thicknesses and textures. Stranded cotton threads can be separated; use two strands for fine work. Use embroidery floss to decorate or to secure fabrics.

Fabric glue This can be used instead of iron-on fusible bonding web to bind fabrics or trimmings together. It should be applied sparingly.

Fabrics Many kinds of fabric can be used in appliqué, and you will often be able to use remnants and other scraps. See the individual projects for advice on which fabrics are suitable for which technique or end use. Fabrics such as cotton can be dyed to obtain the desired color for a particular design.

Felt Because this is a nonwoven fabric, it is easy to cut and does not fray, making it very suitable for appliqué.

Iron-on fusible bonding web This is a very effective material for binding two pieces of fabric together. It consists of a fine web of adhesive that is activated by the heat of an iron (see Basic Techniques). The result is washable and very durable.

Ribbons These are available in a wide variety of colors, materials, patterns and textures. Ribbons can be used functionally as drawstrings or as decoration.

Seam binding This can be used for finishing edges.

Sewing threads These are used to machine-stitch fabrics together or to embellish designs.

Trimmings Many different kinds of trimmings are available, from simple braids to highly decorative pom-poms and fringing.

Yarn Tapestry yarn is a strong matte embroidery thread that works very well on woolen fabrics; use a large-eyed tapestry needle. Knitting yarn can also be used for embroidery or to make your own pom-poms.

1 Beads and buttons
2 Embroidery floss
3 Fabrics
4 Sewing threads
5 Yarn
6 Seam binding
7 Ribbon
8 Felt
9 Trimmings

EQUIPMENT

VERY LITTLE SPECIAL EQUIPMENT IS NEEDED FOR APPLIQUÉ WORK. THE MOST IMPORTANT ITEM IS A SHARP PAIR OF SCISSORS. KEEP SCISSORS USED FOR CUTTING FABRICS AND THREADS SEPARATE FROM THOSE USED FOR PAPER AND CARDBOARD, OTHERWISE THEY QUICKLY WILL BECOME BLUNT.

Beading needle This needle is specially designed for stitching beads onto fabric. It is very fine and flexible and particularly useful for tiny beads.

Dressmaker's pins These are used to pin fabrics together before basting and stitching. Do not use blunt or rusty pins.

Dressmaker's scissors These should be used for cutting only fabric. Do not use them to cut paper or cardboard, as this will blunt the edges.

Embroidery scissors These small scissors are very sharp and are used to trim fabrics and cut threads. Do not use them to cut large areas of fabric.

Fading fabric marker This marker is very useful for drawing designs on fabric. The marks will fade on contact with air or water (see Basic Techniques).

Iron Always check the temperature before ironing different fabrics. If possible, it is a good idea to use a separate iron for iron-on fusible bonding web.

Needle threader This is not essential, but does help when threading hand-sewing needles.

Pencil A pencil is useful for scaling up templates. To mark fabrics, use one of the other materials listed here.

Pinking shears These scissors have serrated blades designed to cut fabrics so that the edges do not fray. They should not be used to cut paper.

Quilting pins These are longer than dressmaker's pins and can pin several layers of fabric and batting together.

Ruler Use a metal ruler to draw straight lines on fabric. You may also need a ruler to enlarge the size of a template.

Safety pins These can be used to hold layers of fabric together. A safety pin is also needed to thread a drawstring through a fabric casing.

Sewing machine A sewing machine with different stitch settings can be used for appliqué. Bobbins can be filled with a different-colored thread from the top thread to create decorative effects. Hand-sewing can then be used for decorative finishes.

Tailor's chalk This is particularly useful to mark dark shades of fabric or those with uneven texture. It will rub off or disappear after washing.

Tape measure This is more flexible than a ruler and is also used to measure lengths of fabric.

1 Pinking shears
2 Tape measure
3 Sewing machine
4 Quilting pins

5 Embroidery scissors
6 Bobbins
7 Needles
8 Needle threader

BASIC TECHNIQUES

THE BASIC IDEA BEHIND APPLIQUÉ IS A VERY SIMPLE ONE: SMALL PIECES OF FABRIC ARE APPLIED TO A BACKGROUND FABRIC TO CREATE DECORATIVE EFFECTS. HOWEVER, THE FOLLOWING TECHNIQUES WILL MAKE THE TASK EASIER AND WILL AID IN THE SUCCESS OF THE FINAL RESULT.

TRANSFERRING ORIGINAL DESIGNS

Tracing Templates

1 Place a piece of tracing paper over the shape. Draw around the shape, using a soft pencil.

2 Remove the tracing paper and turn it over. Scribble over the drawn lines as shown. Turn the tracing paper over again and place it on a piece of paper or thin cardboard. Draw over the original drawing.

3 The shape should now be transferred to the paper or cardboard. Go over it with a pencil if it is faint. Cut out the template.

Enlarging Templates

To enlarge a template, trace it onto graph paper following the instructions above. Decide the scale you want to enlarge it to, then draw it again on a piece of larger-size graph paper. You can also enlarge templates on a photocopier.

Using a Fabric Marker

This is used to draw around a template to transfer the shape to fabric. The marks made by a fading fabric marker gradually disappear on contact with air or water. You can also use a dressmaker's pencil.

Using Tailor's Chalk

This is useful for drawing designs on dark fabric or on fabrics with an uneven texture. The chalk marks wash out or rub off.

IRON-ON FUSIBLE BONDING WEB

1 Set an iron to medium heat. Iron the bonding web onto the reverse side of the fabric.

2 Place the template on the backing paper of the bonding web. Draw around the shape, using a pencil, then cut out with a pair of scissors.

3 Remove the backing paper. Position the shape on the background fabric and iron it in place.

SATIN STITCH APPLIQUÉ

1 Draw the shape you wish to appliqué on a piece of fabric. Pin this onto the background fabric. Machine-stitch around the outline with a straight stitch.

2 Using sharp scissors, trim the excess appliqué fabric, cutting close to the machine stitches.

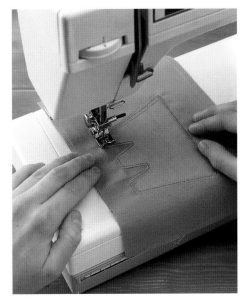

3 Machine-stitch over the first stitched outline and the edge of the shape, using a satin stitch or an embroidery stitch.

TACKING OVER PAPER

1 Draw around the template on a piece of fabric. Cut out, leaving an extra ¼-inch seam allowance, as shown.

2 Cut another paper template and place it on the back of the fabric shape. Baste the seam allowance over the edge of the paper, gently pulling the thread. Snip the fabric at points (for example, at the inner point of a heart design) to help it fold over neatly.

3 Using a hot iron, iron over the back. Carefully remove the basting stitches and the paper template.

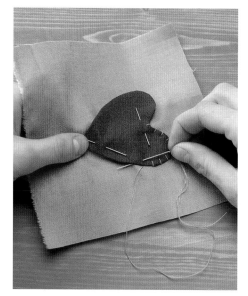

4 Pin the appliqué shape onto the background fabric. Hand- or machine-stitch around the edge.

REVERSE APPLIQUÉ

1 Draw around the template onto the main fabric. Draw another line approximately ¼ inch inside the shape. Using sharp scissors, cut out the inner shape. Clip the ¼-inch border at intervals, then fold back to give a smooth outline. Press in place with a hot iron.

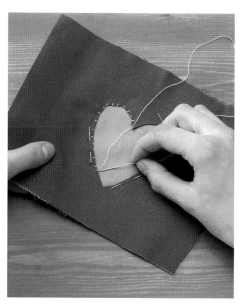

2 Place a contrasting fabric behind the outline shape and pin. Stitch around the edge of the shape.

CUTTING AND FOLDING EDGES

Curves

1 Using a sharp pair of scissors, snip into the dip in the curve up to the marked line. For the outside of the curve, cut out evenly spaced triangular notches of fabric.

Points

1 To make a neat folded point, cut away the fabric around the point, as shown.

Inside Angles

1 At the inner point of the angle, snip the fabric up to the marked line.

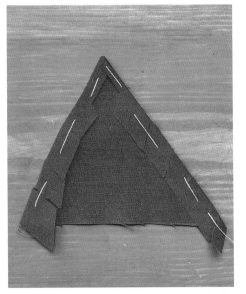

2 Fold over the edge along the marked line to the wrong side. Press with a hot iron, then baste in place.

2 Fold over the edge along the marked line to the wrong side. Press with a hot iron, then baste in place.

2 Fold over the edge along the marked line to the wrong side. Press with a hot iron, then baste in place.

HAND STITCHES

Many different embroidery stitches can be used to attach and embellish appliqué shapes. These are some of the most commonly used hand stitches.

Stab Stitch

Bring the needle through the appliqué shape to the right side of the fabric. Start as close to or as far from the edge as you wish, depending on the size stitch required. Insert the needle into the background fabric to make a straight stitch.

French Knots

Bring the needle through the edge of the appliqué shape to the right side of the fabric. Holding the thread taut with your left hand, twist it several times around the needle. Still holding the thread taut, turn the needle and insert it back through the fabric at the same point. Pull gently on the needle to form a neat knot.

Featherstitch

Starting at a point of the appliqué shape, bring the needle through the edge to the right side of the fabric. Make slanting stitches alternately to left and right, pulling the needle through the loop in the thread with each stitch. The stitches on the left will hold the shape in place.

Blanket Stitch

Work from left to right. Bring the needle through the appliqué shape to the right side of the fabric. Start as close to or as far from the edge as you wish, depending on whether you want a small or large stitch. Work a vertical stitch, catching thread under the tip of the needle as you draw it through the fabric. Space the stitches as evenly as possible.

Running Stitch

This is the simplest handappliqué stitch. Bring the needle through the edge of the appliqué shape to the right side of the fabric. Insert the needle back in the fabric, leaving a gap approximately the same size as the stitch. The stitches can be any size. You can alternate the length of the stitches for decorative effect.

Cross-stitch

Bring the needle through the appliqué shape to the right side of the fabric. Start as close to or as far from the edge as you wish, depending on whether you want a small or large stitch. Insert the needle in the background fabric at an angle. Bring the needle out again on the appliqué shape immediately above this point. Make a stitch in the opposite direction from the first to form a cross.

HEART GIFT DECORATIONS

IT IS ALWAYS SUCH A TREAT TO RECEIVE A HANDMADE CARD AND MATCHING GIFT BOX. IT DOESN'T TAKE A HUGE AMOUNT OF TIME BUT THE RESULT IS SO SPECIAL. THE DESIGNS IN THIS PARTICULAR PROJECT ARE RICH AND SUMPTUOUS IN THEIR COLORS AND FABRICS, WHICH MAKES THEM PERFECT FOR VALENTINE'S DAY, BUT YOU EASILY COULD ADAPT THE IDEA TO SUIT OTHER SPECIAL OCCASIONS USING DIFFERENT COLORS AND MOTIFS.

1 Cut out small hearts from scraps of organza, slightly narrower than the width of the organza ribbon. You will need approximately 20 hearts per yard of ribbon.

2 Sew each heart onto the ribbon with a running stitch using a contrasting thread that will show up against the fabric. Alternate the colors of the hearts along the length of the ribbon.

3 For the gift tag, cut a piece of colored cardboard to the size required and punch a hole at the top. ▶

MATERIALS AND EQUIPMENT YOU WILL NEED

EMBROIDERY SCISSORS • SCRAPS OF ORGANZA FABRICS • ¾-INCH-WIDE ORGANZA RIBBON • NEEDLE AND CONTRASTING SEWING THREADS • PAPER SCISSORS • COLORED CARDBOARD • HOLE PUNCH • EMBROIDERY FLOSS • DOUBLE-SIDED TAPE • DECORATIVE CORD • RULER • ASSORTED BEADS • SMALL GIFT BOX

4 Cut out a heart from organza and lay it on a square of organza in a contrasting color. Lay a third piece of organza over the top. Decorate with stitches using embroidery floss and tape to the tag.

6 For the greeting card, cut a 4 x 5-inch piece of cardboard and fold in half. Use layers of organza to make up the main design, basting the fabric together to hold it in place.

7 Embellish the appliqué with decorative beads and stitches. Attach the appliqué design to the card with double-sided tape as before.

5 Cut a length of decorative cord and thread it through the punched hole. Tie the two ends in a knot.

8 For the gift box, assemble another appliqué design, using a combination of fabrics and basting them in place, as before. Embellish with beads and decorative stitches and attach to the lid with tape.

KITCHEN COLLAGE

Blue and white plain and patterned fabrics make a very attractive fabric collage to hang on the wall of a kitchen or breakfast room. Display the collage as it is, as a small wall hanging, or mount it in a box frame so that the glass does not touch the appliqué. The collage would also work well in shades of another color, such as pink or green, to match your china.

1 Cut two pieces of striped and plain fabric for the background to make an overall size of 13½ x 16½ inches. Machine-stitch together, then cover the seam with fabric tape. Fold under the edges by ½ inch and press. Pin in place.

2 Iron fusible bonding web onto the reverse side of scraps of plain and patterned fabrics.

3 Trace the coffeepot and cup shapes from the back of the book and make templates (see Basic Techniques). Draw around the templates onto the bonding web and cut out.

MATERIALS AND EQUIPMENT YOU WILL NEED

DRESSMAKER'S SCISSORS • STRIPED AND PLAIN COTTON FABRICS • SEWING MACHINE AND MATCHING THREADS • FABRIC TAPE • IRON •
DRESSMAKER'S PINS • IRON-ON FUSIBLE BONDING WEB • SCRAPS OF PLAIN AND PATTERNED FABRICS • TRACING PAPER • SOFT PENCIL •
PAPER OR THIN CARDBOARD • PAPER SCISSORS • FADING FABRIC MARKER • EMBROIDERY SCISSORS • NEEDLE • EMBROIDERY FLOSS •
SMALL POM-POM (OPTIONAL) • BUTTONS • POM-POM TRIMMING • CRAFT KNIFE • MAT BOARD • DOUBLE-SIDED ADHESIVE TAPE

4 Peel off the backing paper from the coffeepot shape and position on the fabric background. Iron in place. Repeat steps 1–4 for the coffee cup.

6 Work a swirl in running stitch on the top of the coffee cup to indicate steam. Stitch a wavy line of running stitches to indicate steam coming out of the spout of the coffeepot.

7 Stitch the pom-pom trimming along the bottom edge of the picture, as shown, so that the pom-poms show on the right side.   ▶

5 Decorate the appliqué with simple stitches. Outline some of the shapes with a stab stitch or blanket stitch to accentuate them. Sew a small pom-pom or button onto the lid of the coffeepot.

Simple decorative hand stitches complement the country-style design.

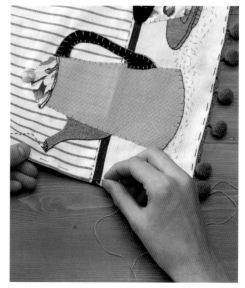

8 Hand-stitch neatly around the folded edges of the picture.

10 To frame the appliqué, cut a piece of matte board large enough to leave a wide border all around the picture. Attach the appliqué with a strip of double-sided tape along the top edge. Sign the picture in pencil.

9 Sew a decorative button at each corner.

ALPHABET APRON

LARGE, BOLD SHAPES AND BRIGHT COLORS ARE IDEAL FOR THIS CHILD'S APRON. THE COTTON FABRICS ARE STRONGLY STITCHED WITH DOUBLE SEAMS AND ZIGZAG-STITCHING, SO THE APRON WILL STAND UP TO PLENTY OF WEAR AND FREQUENT WASHING.

1 Fold the main fabrics in half horizontally. With the wrong sides facing and the center points matching, pin together along one side. Machine-stitch, fold over the seam and stitch again. Mark curves at the top corners, as shown, and cut. Hem the edges.

2 Enlarge the letters from the back of the book to approximately 2¾ inches high (see Basic Techniques). Reverse and make templates.

3 Draw around the letters on the backing of the fusible bonding web. Iron the bonding web onto the reverse of the scraps of fabric, using different colors for adjacent letters, and cut out.

4 Arrange the letters in five rows on the apron fabrics. Peel off the backing paper and iron in place.

5 Using matching threads, zigzag-stitch around the edges of the letters.

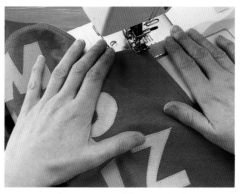

6 Cut the tape or ribbon into four equal lengths. Machine-stitch to the top sides of the apron and either side of the neck edge. Knot the neck ties together and adjust to fit.

MATERIALS AND EQUIPMENT YOU WILL NEED

16 x 28-INCH RECTANGLE RED COTTON FABRIC • 12 x 16-INCH RECTANGLE BLUE COTTON FABRIC • DRESSMAKER'S PINS •
SEWING MACHINE AND MATCHING THREADS • TAILOR'S CHALK • DRESSMAKER'S SCISSORS • TRACING PAPER • SOFT PENCIL • GRAPH PAPER •
PAPER OR THIN CARDBOARD • PAPER SCISSORS • IRON-ON FUSIBLE BONDING WEB • IRON • SCRAPS OF COTTON FABRICS, IN BRIGHT COLORS •
EMBROIDERY SCISSORS • 60 INCHES OF ¼-INCH-WIDE YELLOW FABRIC TAPE OR RIBBON

HANDS AND HEARTS THROW

USE YOUR OWN HAND AS THE TEMPLATE FOR THIS TRADITIONAL QUILTED THROW. THE SYMBOLIC MOTIFS AND COTTON CHECK FABRICS, BORROWED FROM AMERICAN FOLK DESIGNS, GENERATE A FEELING OF WARMTH AND HOSPITALITY. IN THIS PROJECT, THE BUTTONS ARE NOT SIMPLY FOR DECORATION; THEY SERVE TO QUILT THE LAYERS OF FABRIC TOGETHER. LAY THE THROW FLAT FOR QUILTING AND WORK FROM THE CENTER OUTWARD.

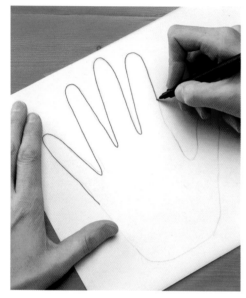

1 Draw around your hand with pencil. Draw around the outline again using a felt pen, simplifying the shape.

2 Trace the hand shape and transfer it to the paper side of the fusible bonding web (see Basic Techniques). Iron the bonding web onto the reverse of a piece of check fabric and cut out.

3 Draw a heart shape on bonding web. Iron the bonding web onto the reverse of a piece of contrasting fabric and cut out. Iron the heart onto the hand, as shown. ▶

MATERIALS AND EQUIPMENT YOU WILL NEED

SOFT PENCIL • PAPER • FELT-TIP PEN • TRACING PAPER • IRON-ON FUSIBLE BONDING WEB • DRESSMAKER'S SCISSORS • IRON • SCRAPS OF COTTON CHECK FABRICS, IN DIFFERENT COLORS • 60-INCH SQUARE OF HEAVY COTTON CREAM FABRIC • DRESSMAKER'S PINS • SEWING MACHINE AND MATCHING THREADS • 64-INCH SQUARE OF COTTON CHECK FABRIC, FOR THE BACKING • 60-INCH SQUARE OF POLYESTER BATTING • SAFETY PINS • STRANDED COTTON EMBROIDERY FLOSS • NEEDLE • ASSORTED BUTTONS

4 Make 11 more hand shapes, varying the fabrics. Iron a heart shape onto each hand, as in step 3. Peel off the backing paper.

6 Using matching threads, machine-stitch around both the hand and the heart shapes in a close zigzag stitch.

8 Press under ½ inch of the backing fabric all around. Fold over to the right side of the throw and press under 2 inches to make a border. Pin, then machine-stitch, mitering the corners. Using six strands of embroidery floss, sew buttons between the hand shapes.

5 Position the hands on the cream fabric, leaving a border of approximately 10 inches all around. Pin in place, then iron.

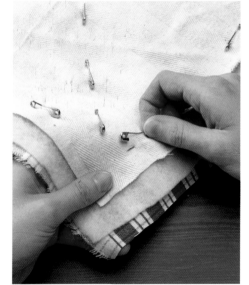

7 Lay the backing fabric out flat, with the wrong side facing upward. Center the batting on top. Lay the appliqué right side up on top. Trim the batting so that the backing fabric is 2½ inches larger all around. Secure the three layers together with safety pins.

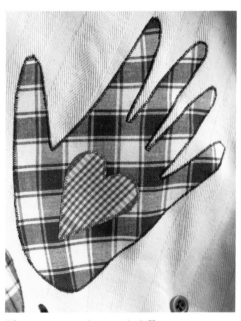

The secret to working with different patterns is to choose a limited range of colors.

ANGEL STOCKING

Different shades of dark blue and faded denim work very well together, showing that you do not always need to use bright or contrasting colors in appliqué. This is a good way to recycle old jeans and denim shirts. Make the Christmas stocking as large or as small as you wish—the denim fabric is certainly strong enough to carry the weight of plenty of presents!

1 Trace the angel shapes at the back of the book and make templates (see Basic Techniques). Iron fusible bonding web onto the back of scraps of denim. Draw around the templates on the bonding web and cut out.

2 Draw a large stocking shape on a piece of paper and cut out to make a template. Draw around the template on two pieces of denim and cut out. Remove the backing paper from the bonding web. Position the appliqué shapes on the right side of one stocking piece and iron in place.

3 Decorate the angel with different embroidery stitches, as shown. Stitch the features on the face and the hair.

4 Sew buttons around the angel and scattered over the rest of the stocking. ▶

MATERIALS AND EQUIPMENT YOU WILL NEED

TRACING PAPER • SOFT PENCIL • PAPER OR THIN CARDBOARD • PAPER SCISSORS • IRON • IRON-ON FUSIBLE BONDING WEB • SCRAPS OF DENIM, IN DIFFERENT SHADES • DRESSMAKER'S PENCIL OR FADING FABRIC MARKER • DRESSMAKER'S SCISSORS • NEEDLE • EMBROIDERY FLOSS • BUTTONS • DRESSMAKER'S PINS • RIBBON • SEWING MACHINE AND MATCHING THREADS • PINKING SHEARS • GINGHAM FABRIC

5 With the right sides facing, pin the two stocking pieces together, leaving the top edge open. Cut a 4¾-inch length of ribbon, fold in half and trap between the two stocking pieces on one side, approximately 2½ inches below the top. Machine-stitch the pieces, leaving a ½-inch seam. Neaten the raw edges with pinking shears.

7 Place the denim stocking inside the lining stocking, matching the top raw edges. Pin the denim and lining together around the top opening. Machine-stitch, leaving a ½-inch seam.

6 For the lining, use pinking shears to cut two stocking shapes from gingham fabric. With the right sides facing, pin together, leaving the top edge open. Machine-stitch, leaving a ½-inch seam and a 6-inch gap along one side.

8 Push the denim stocking through the gap in the lining, then push the lining inside the denim stocking. Slip-stitch the gap. Stitch a line of running stitch around the top edge of the stocking. Make additional stockings in the same way, varying the designs.

TOY BAG

Stow away toys or laundry in this strong cotton drill bag. The appliqué dog motif is made of different scraps of leftover fabrics, ironed in place with fusible bonding web. For wet laundry or sports clothes, you can make a plastic lining to go inside the bag.

1 With the right sides facing, fold the cotton drill fabric in half horizontally. Machine-stitch the side seams, stopping 10 inches from the top. Reverse-stitch to reinforce the stitching. Fold back the top edges by 4 inches so that the right sides are facing. Stitch, leaving a ½-inch seam allowance, and fold right side out. Turn the bag right side out.

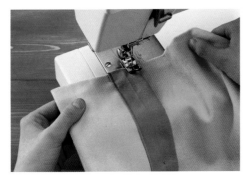

2 To make the casings for the ribbon ties, cut two strips of contrasting fabric. Fold in half lengthwise and press. Open out, then fold the sides into the center. Fold over each end. Position one on each side of the bag and stitch in place, leaving one end open. Cut a second piece of contrasting fabric 9 x 8¼ inches. Fold under ¼ inch on each side and press.

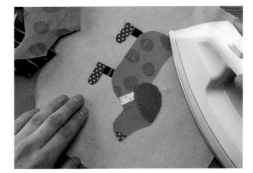

3 Trace the dog shapes from the back of the book and make templates (see Basic Techniques). Iron the fusible bonding web onto the reverse side of scraps of different fabrics. Draw around the templates on the bonding web and cut out. Position the dog shapes on the fabric panel and iron in place.

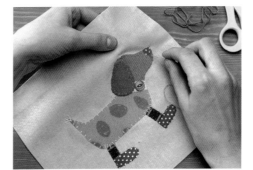

4 Stitch on a bead for the dog's eye and embroider French knots for the nose. Stitch a button on the collar.

5 Position the panel on one side of the bag and pin in place. Machine-stitch. Stitch a button to each corner by hand.

6 Cut the ribbon in half. Fasten a safety pin to one end of one ribbon, then thread it through the casing. Secure at either end with pins. Thread the second ribbon through the other casing and pin the ends. Cut each felt square into two triangles. Trap each pair of ribbon ends between two triangles, then stitch all around the edge with a running stitch.

MATERIALS AND EQUIPMENT YOU WILL NEED

DRESSMAKER'S SCISSORS • 20 x 60-INCH RECTANGLE COTTON DRILL FABRIC, FOR THE BAG • SEWING MACHINE AND MATCHING THREADS •
TWO PLAIN, CONTRASTING FABRICS • IRON • TRACING PAPER • SOFT PENCIL • PAPER OR THIN CARDBOARD • PAPER SCISSORS •
IRON-ON FUSIBLE BONDING WEB • SCRAPS OF DIFFERENT FABRICS • NEEDLE AND EMBROIDERY FLOSS • EMBROIDERY SCISSORS • BEAD • BUTTONS •
DRESSMAKER'S PINS • 3 YARDS NARROW RIBBON • SAFETY PINS • TWO 4-INCH SQUARES OF FELT, IN DIFFERENT COLORS

HEARTS AND STARS BLANKET

THIS BRIGHTLY DECORATED BLANKET IS CERTAIN TO CHEER YOU UP AS WELL AS KEEP YOU WARM. ITS APPEAL LIES IN THE TONING ICE-CREAM COLORS AND TEXTURED FABRIC. THE APPLIQUÉ MOTIFS ARE ALL MADE OF BLANKET FABRIC STITCHED BY HAND WITH YARN, WHICH GIVES A BOLD, CHUNKY FEEL TO THE DESIGN. IF YOU ARE MAKING THE BLANKET FOR A CHILD, LEAVE OUT THE BEADS AND BUTTONS AND USE EXTRA EMBROIDERY STITCHES AS EMBELLISHMENT INSTEAD.

1 Trace the heart and star templates from the back of the book and make templates (see Basic Techniques). Draw around the templates on the colored blanket fabrics using a fading fabric marker and cut out.

2 Embroider some of the hearts and stars with French knots, using yarn in contrasting colors (see Basic Techniques).

3 Embroider the remaining hearts and stars with decorative cross-stitches in contrasting colors.

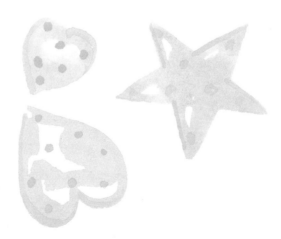

MATERIALS AND EQUIPMENT YOU WILL NEED

TRACING PAPER • SOFT PENCIL • PAPER OR THIN CARDBOARD • PAPER SCISSORS • SCRAPS OF COLORED BLANKET FABRIC • FADING FABRIC MARKER • DRESSMAKER'S SCISSORS • TAPESTRY NEEDLE • TAPESTRY YARN OR KNITTING YARN, IN DIFFERENT COLORS • ASSORTED BEADS • SMALL, COLORED BUTTONS • BLANKET • DRESSMAKER'S PINS

4 Stitch assorted beads onto some of the appliqué shapes. Be careful to attach them securely.

6 Work a line of decorative running stitch along each end of the blanket in contrasting wool.

7 Lay the blanket out flat and position the heart and star shapes in a pleasing arrangement. Pin them in place. ▶

5 Stitch buttons to the other shapes and embroider with more decorative stitches, using yarn.

Buttons and beads add interest to the appliqué shape.

8 Stitch some of the shapes onto the blanket, using a stab stitch (see Basic Techniques) and a contrasting yarn.

10 Fill in the background with individual large cross-stitches.

9 Stitch the remaining shapes onto the blanket, using a blanket stitch.

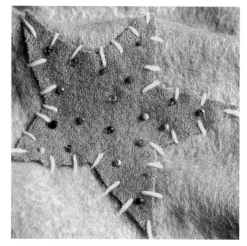

A stab stitch is decorative and holds the appliqué shape in place.

MOSAIC VELVET CUSHION

THIS RICH VELVET CUSHION COVER IS A CLEVER WAY TO USE SCRAPS OF FABRIC. THE TRIANGULAR SHAPES AND DECORATIVE EMBROIDERY ARE REMINISCENT OF CRAZY PATCHWORK, WHICH WAS VERY POPULAR IN THE VICTORIAN ERA. THE AIM AT THE TIME WAS TO CREATE A RANDOM DESIGN, HENCE THE NAME. TO CREATE A MOSAIC EFFECT, THE PIECES MAY BE ARRANGED MORE REGULARLY. TO MAKE THE CUSHION, SEE THE INLAID BOAT CUSHION PROJECT.

1 Measure the cushion pad. For the cushion front, cut a piece of velvet to this size plus ¾ inch all around. Cut triangles in different sizes from scraps of contrasting velvet. Press under the edges of the triangles by ½ inch, making sure that the edges are straight.

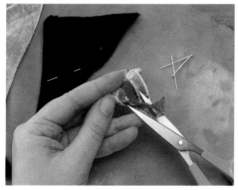

2 Trim the excess fabric at the corners. Baste around the edge of each triangle. Arrange the triangles on the background velvet and pin in place.

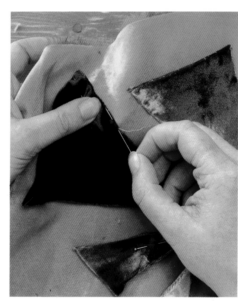

3 Slip-stitch neatly around the edge of each triangle. Remove basting thread.

4 Outline some of the triangles with a featherstitch, using contrasting embroidery floss.

5 Stitch around the edge of other triangles with a blanket stitch and other decorative embroidery stitches. Make the cushion and insert the pad.

MATERIALS AND EQUIPMENT YOU WILL NEED

TAPE MEASURE • CUSHION PAD • DRESSMAKER'S SCISSORS • VELVET • SCRAPS OF CONTRASTING VELVET • IRON • EMBROIDERY SCISSORS • NEEDLE • BASTING THREAD • DRESSMAKER'S PINS • MATCHING SEWING THREADS • EMBROIDERY FLOSS

COUNTRY CANDLE SHADES

NATURAL-COLORED LINEN AND TEXTURED APPLIQUÉ FABRICS COMPLEMENT ONE ANOTHER IN THESE CHARMING CANDLE SHADES. FRAY THE EDGES OF THE FABRICS AND DECORATE THE DESIGN WITH PEARL BUTTONS AND EMBROIDERY STITCHES TO COMPLETE THE EFFECT. IN THIS PROJECT, THE CARDBOARD TEMPLATE IS USED IN THE FINISHED CANDLE SHADE TO BACK THE APPLIQUÉ. DO NOT LEAVE THE CANDLE SHADES UNATTENDED AT ANY TIME WHILE IN USE.

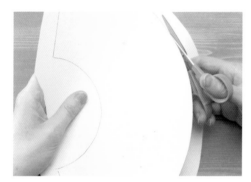

1 Enlarge the candle shade shape from the back of the book so that it measures 4 inches high (see Basic Techniques). Transfer to thin cardboard and cut out to make a template.

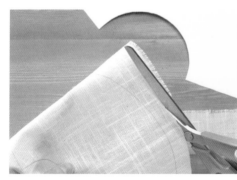

2 Using a fading fabric marker, draw around the template on the linen fabric. Cut out the fabric, adding an extra ½ inch for turnings.

3 Draw small heart shapes on scraps of fabric and cut out. Cut small squares of fabric and fray the edges slightly. Appliqué some of the heart shapes through the squares onto the candle shade fabric, using a stab stitch and two strands of embroidery floss.

4 Add the single heart shapes. Sew pearl buttons in the middle of some of the appliqué hearts and scattered over the background. Vary the stitches used.

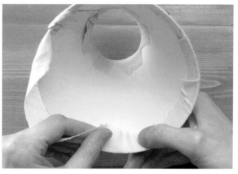

5 Place the appliquéd shade face down on a protected surface and spray lightly with adhesive. Place the cardboard template on top. Fold the edges of the linen to the inside, smoothing the fabric as you go.

6 Fold in the raw edge and glue lightly. Bend the candle shade into shape and hold together with paper clips until the glue is dry. Slip-stitch the attached edge if necessary, stitching through the cardboard.

MATERIALS AND EQUIPMENT YOU WILL NEED
TRACING PAPER • SOFT PENCIL • GRAPH PAPER • THIN CARDBOARD • PAPER SCISSORS • FADING FABRIC MARKER •
10 x 14-INCH RECTANGLE NATURAL-COLORED LINEN • DRESSMAKER'S SCISSORS • SCRAPS OF NATURAL-COLORED AND TEXTURED FABRICS •
EMBROIDERY SCISSORS • NEEDLE • STRANDED COTTON EMBROIDERY FLOSS • SMALL PEARL BUTTONS • CRAFT ADHESIVE SPRAY •
FABRIC GLUE • PAPER CLIPS

CHRISTMAS TREE STARS

Red and green, the traditional festive colors, are mixed and matched in these two complementary designs. Both are simple and quick to make by hand, using small, neat running stitches. As an alternative to this bold, coordinated effect, you can experiment with a variety of different colors or embellish the Christmas decorations with beads, sequins and shiny embroidery floss.

1 Draw a star shape on paper or thin cardboard and make a template. Using tailor's chalk, draw around the template onto felt.

2 Cut equal numbers of red and green stars from the felt.

3 Using the point of the scissors, pierce one of the red stars ½ inch from the edge. Cut out a smaller star, leaving a ½-inch border all around. ▶

MATERIALS AND EQUIPMENT YOU WILL NEED
SOFT PENCIL • PAPER OR THIN CARDBOARD • PAPER SCISSORS • TAILOR'S CHALK • RED AND GREEN FELT • EMBROIDERY SCISSORS •
NEEDLE AND MATCHING THREADS • SCRAPS OF PATTERNED FABRIC • RIBBON

4 Stitch the red border to one of the green stars with small, even running stitches and matching thread.

6 Place the stars from steps 4 and 5 together, sandwiching a plain red star in the middle. Stitch the three stars together at the inner points, as shown.

8 Stitch the two stars together around the edges with a stab stitch.

5 Center a small red star cut out in step 3 on a green star. Stitch in place.

7 For a different decoration, take a green felt star and cut a small circle from the center. Place on top of a red star, with a small piece of patterned fabric showing through the hole. Stitch neatly around the hole in a running stitch.

9 Use a loop of ribbon for hanging. Alternatively, wrap sewing thread around all four fingers. Stitch a loop onto a point of each star with small stitches.

INLAID BOAT CUSHION

INLAID APPLIQUÉ IS A VARIATION ON THE BASIC TECHNIQUE IN WHICH THE DESIGN IS DRAWN ON THE BACKGROUND FABRIC AND CUT OUT, LEAVING OPEN SPACES. THE CUTOUT SHAPES ARE THEN PLACED ON FABRICS OF CONTRASTING COLORS AND CUT OUT AGAIN, AND THE CONTRASTING COLORED SHAPES ARE USED TO FILL THE SPACES. THIS TECHNIQUE IS BEST SUITED TO FABRICS OF THE SAME THICKNESS THAT DO NOT FRAY, SUCH AS BLANKET AND HEAVY WOOLEN FABRICS.

1 Trace the templates from the back of the book and enlarge to the size required (see Basic Techniques). Measure the cushion pad and cut out a piece of blanket fabric to this size plus ¾ inch all around. Position the templates on the main fabric. Using a fading fabric marker, draw around the templates on the reverse side of the fabric.

2 Using a pair of sharp scissors, cut out the shapes from the main fabric.

3 Place each cutout shape on a piece of different-colored blanket fabric, pin and cut out. ▶

MATERIALS AND EQUIPMENT YOU WILL NEED

TRACING PAPER • SOFT PENCIL • PAPER OR THIN CARDBOARD • PAPER SCISSORS • TAPE MEASURE • SQUARE CUSHION PAD • DRESSMAKER'S SCISSORS • BLANKET FABRICS IN DIFFERENT COLORS • FADING FABRIC MARKER • DRESSMAKER'S PINS • EMBROIDERY SCISSORS • CONTRASTING COTTON FABRICS FOR THE BACK • FABRIC GLUE AND BRUSH • TAPESTRY NEEDLE • YARNS • NEEDLE AND SEWING THREAD • SCRAP OF FELT • CORD • LARGE BUTTON • BEADS • NARROW RIBBON • IRON • FOUR POM-POMS • SEWING MACHINE

4 Cut a piece of cotton fabric larger than the boat design. Glue onto the back of the piece in step 1, behind the cutout areas.

6 Use colored yarns to decorate the sails with French knots (see Basic Techniques) and an appliqué star cut from a scrap of felt.

8 To line the design, cut a piece of cotton fabric the same size as the cushion front and place it on the reverse of the appliqué. For the cushion back, cut two pieces of fabric in different colors, to the width of the front but two-thirds of the length. Fold under and press a ½-inch double hem on both opening edges; machine-stitch. With the right sides facing, place the cushion front on the two overlapping back pieces and machine-stitch all around. Turn the cushion cover right side out. Hand-stitch a pom-pom to each corner.

5 Place the colored cutout shapes in the openings and pin in place. Using colored yarns, hand-stitch the shapes to the surrounding blanket with large stab stitches.

7 Cut a small fabric rectangle for the cabin and appliqué in place, as shown. Using sewing thread, stitch on a piece of cord for the mast, add a large button at the top, then stitch ribbon across the boat's hull, using a cross-stitch. Sew a bead to the bottom corner of each sail.

SHADOW-APPLIQUÉ SCARF

THIS DELICATE, FLOATY SCARF IS MADE OF LAYERS OF CHIFFON, WITH SQUARES OF FABRIC APPLIQUÉD AT RANDOM WITH A LEAFLIKE MOTIF. CHIFFON IS A RATHER SLIPPERY FABRIC, SO IT PAYS TO BASTE THE LAYERS SECURELY TOGETHER BEFORE MACHINE-STITCHING. THE RAW EDGES OF THE APPLIQUÉ ARE FINISHED WITH EMBROIDERY STITCHES, AND THE EDGES OF THE SCARF ARE ROLLED AND STITCHED BY HAND.

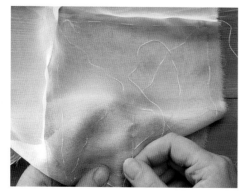

1 Cut a 12 x 41-inch piece of chiffon. Press in half lengthwise, open out, then press folds 6 inches along the length. Cut 6¾-inch squares of chiffon. Baste one square to the reverse of the main piece, using fold lines as a guide.

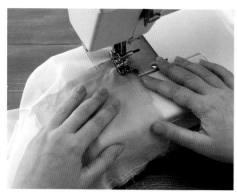

2 Following the fold lines, machine-stitch the square in place. Trim the excess fabric ⅛ inch outside the stitch line. Repeat along the scarf.

3 Make leaf and circle templates. Using a fading fabric marker, draw around the templates several times on different squares of chiffon.

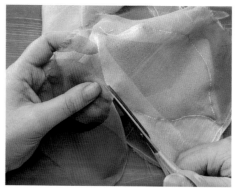

4 Pin each appliqué square onto a contrasting square on the scarf, choosing squares at random. Baste, then machine-stitch around the shape. Trim the excess fabric ⅛ inch outside the stitch line.

5 Using doubled sewing thread, stitch along all the machine-stitched lines in featherstitch to cover the raw edges.

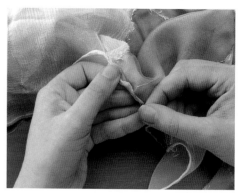

6 Using your forefinger and thumb, carefully roll each edge of the scarf until the raw edges are concealed. Stitch in place with a slip-stitch.

MATERIALS AND EQUIPMENT YOU WILL NEED

DRESSMAKER'S SCISSORS • CHIFFON, IN THREE DIFFERENT COLORS • IRON • DRESSMAKER'S PINS • NEEDLE • BASTING THREAD • SEWING MACHINE AND MATCHING THREADS • SOFT PENCIL • PAPER OR THIN CARDBOARD • PAPER SCISSORS • FADING FABRIC MARKER • EMBROIDERY SCISSORS

HEARTWARMING HATS

BRIGHTEN UP A COLD WINTER'S DAY WITH THESE CHEERFUL APPLIQUÉ HEARTS AND FLOWERS, STITCHED ONTO TWO READY-MADE WOOL HATS AND A SCARF. DECORATE THE SIMPLE SHAPES WITH BEADS, BUTTONS AND EMBROIDERY FLOSS, USING ODDS AND ENDS FROM YOUR NEEDLEWORK BOX. USE A COOL IRON FOR WOOLEN FABRICS AND TAKE CARE NOT TO STRETCH OR DISTORT THEM WHEN YOU STITCH ON THE APPLIQUÉ SHAPES.

1 For the button-heart hat, draw a large heart shape on paper or cardboard and cut out to make a template. Draw around the template on a piece of fusible bonding web. Iron onto a piece of felt and cut out.

2 Position the heart on the front of the hat. Iron in place, using a cool iron.

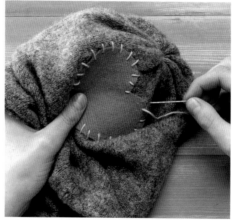

3 Using embroidery floss in a contrasting color, stitch around the edge of the heart in a stab stitch.

4 Decorate the heart with buttons in different sizes and colors.

MATERIALS AND EQUIPMENT YOU WILL NEED

PENCIL • PAPER OR THIN CARDBOARD • PAPER SCISSORS • IRON-ON FUSIBLE BONDING WEB • EMBROIDERY SCISSORS • IRON • SCRAPS OF FELT • WOOL HATS • NEEDLE • EMBROIDERY FLOSS • VARIOUS BUTTONS, IN DIFFERENT SIZES AND COLORS • TRACING PAPER • FADING FABRIC MARKER • WOOLEN SCARF • BEADING NEEDLE • SMALL GLASS BEADS • YARN • STRING

5 For the flowery scarf, draw two flower shapes on paper or thin cardboard and cut out. Using a fading fabric marker, draw around both templates on scraps of felt.

7 Thread a beading needle and knot the end of the thread. Thread on a few beads and stitch down in the center of a flower. Decorate all the flowers in the same way.

9 For the heart hat with pom-pom, draw two heart shapes on paper or cardboard, one smaller than the other. Cut out to make templates. Iron fusible bonding web onto scraps of felt. Draw around the templates several times on the bonding web and cut out. Place the larger heart shapes around the edge of the hat and iron in place, then place smaller hearts on top and iron in place.

6 Position the flowers at either end of the scarf. Using embroidery floss, attach with a few stitches in the center of each flower.

8 Stitch short lengths of embroidery floss in the spaces between the flowers, using a single running stitch. Tie the ends in a double knot, then trim.

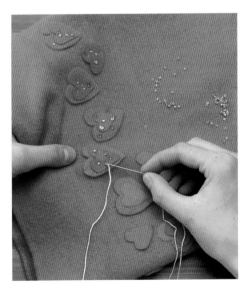

10 Decorate the hearts with stitches and beads, using embroidery flosses in contrasting colors.

▶

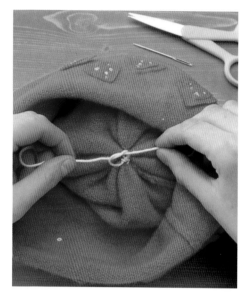

11 To make the pom-pom, cut two 4¾-inch-diameter circles from cardboard. Cut out a 1½-inch-diameter circle from the center of each. Place the two together and wrap yarn around them and through the hole until the central hole is filled. Insert the blades of a sharp pair of scissors between the two pieces of cardboard and cut the yarn. Pass a piece of string between the two pieces of cardboard and knot. Remove the cardboard circles.

12 Fluff up the pom-pom to make a ball, then trim. Stitch to the top of the hat.

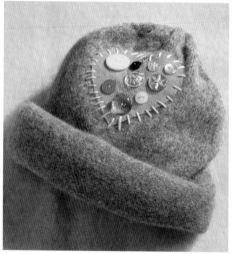

A heart embellished with buttons makes a contemporary decoration.

SPOTTED CUSHION

THE DIFFERENT TEXTURES OF TOWELING, VELVET AND WOOL COME TOGETHER IN THIS VERY ORIGINAL APPLIQUÉ CUSHION. THE CIRCLES ARE CUT OUT AND THEN FILLED IN WITH DIFFERENT FABRICS FROM BEHIND, USING THE REVERSE APPLIQUÉ TECHNIQUE (SEE BASIC TECHNIQUES). THE STITCHING IN THIS PROJECT IS DONE BY MACHINE, EXCEPT FOR THE POM-POM EDGING. IF YOU CANNOT FIND A TRIMMING IN A SUITABLE COLOR, TRY DYEING ONE WITH FABRIC DYE.

1 Measure the cushion pad and cut a piece of wool fabric to this size plus ¾ inch all around. Using tailor's chalk, draw around a circular object on six squares of the same fabric, as shown.

2 Position the squares on the large piece of wool fabric, not too close to the edge. Pin in place.

3 Machine-stitch around each circle in a straight stitch. Remove the pins.

4 Using sharp scissors, cut through both layers of fabric inside each circle close to the stitching. Push the rest of the fabric square through the hole and press in place. Cut out squares of velvet and toweling in different colors, larger than the holes. Pin a fabric square behind each hole, then machine-stitch around the edge of the circle.

5 To make the cushion back, cut two pieces of fabric in different colors to the width of the front and two-thirds of the length. Use pinking shears if desired. Fold under and press a ½-inch double hem on both opening edges. Machine-stitch. Right sides facing, place the cushion front on the two overlapping back pieces and stitch all around.

6 Turn the cushion cover right side out. Hand-stitch the pom-pom trimming around the edge. Insert the cushion pad.

MATERIALS AND EQUIPMENT YOU WILL NEED

TAPE MEASURE • CUSHION PAD • DRESSMAKER'S SCISSORS • WOOL FABRIC • TAILOR'S CHALK • CIRCULAR TEMPLATE • DRESSMAKER'S PINS • SEWING MACHINE AND MATCHING THREADS • EMBROIDERY SCISSORS • IRON • SCRAPS OF VELVET AND TOWELING, IN DIFFERENT COLORS • TWO FABRICS IN DIFFERENT COLORS, FOR THE BACK • PINKING SHEARS (OPTIONAL) • POM-POM TRIMMING • NEEDLE AND MATCHING THREAD

GARDENER'S APRON

MODERN TECHNOLOGY AND TRADITIONAL CRAFT MEET IN THIS STRIKING DESIGN, WHICH MAKES USE OF A HEAT-TRANSFER MACHINE AT A PHOTO-COPYING SHOP. YOU CAN USE IMAGES FROM MAGAZINES OR PHOTOGRAPHS TO CREATE YOUR OWN PERSONALIZED APRON, PERHAPS FOR A COOK OR AN ARTIST. YOU CAN USE IMAGE-TRANSFER GEL INSTEAD OF THE HEAT-TRANSFER MACHINE IN STEP 2. LET THE PRINTS COOL AND DRY BEFORE FOLDING OR MOVING THEM.

1 Cut a selection of flower images out of magazines and photographs. Glue them lightly onto the blank paper.

3 Using a cool iron, iron fusible bonding web onto the reverse of the flower-print fabric.

4 Cut out the flower shapes and arrange on the apron. Peel off the backing paper and iron in place, using a cool iron and protecting the flowers under a piece of cotton fabric.

2 Take the cotton fabric to a photo-copying shop with a heat-transfer machine. Transfer the images to the fabric. Let cool.

5 Stitch around the outline of each flower, using a stab stitch and matching sewing threads.

MATERIALS AND EQUIPMENT YOU WILL NEED

PAPER SCISSORS • FLOWER IMAGES FROM MAGAZINES OR PHOTOGRAPHS • PAPER GLUE • SHEET OF BLANK PAPER • WHITE COTTON FABRIC • IRON •
IRON-ON FUSIBLE BONDING WEB • EMBROIDERY SCISSORS • APRON • NEEDLE • MATCHING SEWING THREADS

FELT CURTAIN

THIS BOLD ABSTRACT DESIGN CAN BRIGHTEN A WINDOW OR BE USED TO DISGUISE AN UNTIDY CORNER. MACHINE-STITCHED STRIPES ARE OVERLAID WITH COLORFUL CIRCLES, AND ATTACHED WITH LARGE HAND STITCHES. THE FELT FABRICS WILL NOT FRAY, SO THERE IS NO NEED TO WORRY ABOUT FINISHING THE EDGES OF ANY OF THE SHAPES. MAKE THE CURTAIN TO FIT THE AREA DESIRED; A LARGER VERSION WOULD MAKE A GOOD ROOM DIVIDER.

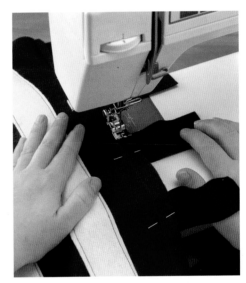

1 Measure the blue felt and cut to the size required for the curtain. Cut the cream felt into strips 1½ inches wide, then pin onto the blue felt 1½ inches apart. Using blue thread, machine-stitch down each side.

2 To make hanging loops, cut a piece of blue felt 4¾ inches wide and the width of the curtain. Using tailor's chalk, mark every 1½ inches. Cut down each marked line to the last, then cut out every other bar. Leaving a 1½-inch band, cut the bottom.

3 Pin the hanging loops to the top of the curtain at the back, then stitch. ▶

MATERIALS AND EQUIPMENT YOU WILL NEED
TAPE MEASURE • BLUE FELT • DRESSMAKER'S SCISSORS • METAL RULER • CREAM FELT • DRESSMAKER'S PINS •
SEWING MACHINE AND MATCHING THREADS • TAILOR'S CHALK • EMBROIDERY SCISSORS • SCRAPS OF COLORED FELT •
CUTTING COMPASS AND MAT (OPTIONAL) • NEEDLE • EMBROIDERY FLOSS

4 Cut out circles of colored felt, using a cutting compass and mat or scissors. Cut out a hole in each circle and swap the colors.

6 Pin the circles to the right side of the curtain. Hand-stitch in place, using contrasting flosses and large, simple stitches.

8 For the border, cut three lengths of blue felt 1½ inches wide, two lengths for the sides and one for the bottom of the curtain. Pin and machine-stitch in place.

5 Using contrasting threads and large, simple stitches, stitch the contrasting centers into the circles.

7 Fold the hanging loops over to the front of the curtain. Stitch in place with small felt circles, using a single large cross-stitch.

BRODERIE PERSE TABLECLOTH

THE IDEA OF CUTTING MOTIFS OUT OF PRINTED FABRICS AND APPLIQUÉING THEM ONTO PLAIN FABRIC CAN BE SEEN IN EARLY QUILTS. IMPORTED CHINTZ FABRICS FROM THE FAR EAST WERE TOO HIGHLY PRIZED TO BE THROWN AWAY AFTER USE, SO THE BEST PORTIONS WERE SAVED AND RECYCLED IN THIS WAY. FOR THE APPLIQUÉ MOTIFS, CHOOSE FABRICS THAT DO NOT FRAY OR PAINT THE EDGES WITH ANTIFRAYING SOLUTION, AVAILABLE FROM CRAFT SHOPS.

1 Fold the tablecloth into quarters and mark 10 inches from the center on each crease with a pin. Unfold the tablecloth. Using a tape measure and the pins as a guide, pin a 20-inch square in the center.

2 Use a pair of embroidery scissors to cut motifs from the printed fabric. The motifs can be cut out fairly roughly at this stage.

3 Iron fusible bonding web onto the reverse of the motifs. Cut them out carefully, as close to the outlines as possible. If necessary, treat the edges with antifraying solution. ▶

MATERIALS AND EQUIPMENT YOU WILL NEED

PLAIN TABLECLOTH • TAPE MEASURE • DRESSMAKER'S PINS • EMBROIDERY SCISSORS • PRINTED FABRIC, WITH SUITABLE MOTIFS • IRON •
IRON-ON FUSIBLE BONDING WEB • ANTIFRAYING SOLUTION (OPTIONAL) • CARDBOARD • SEWING MACHINE AND MATCHING SEWING THREADS •

4 Arrange some of the motifs along the inside edge of the marked square.

6 Using matching threads, machine-stitch around the edge of each motif with a close zigzag stitch.

5 Arrange the rest of the motifs within the marked square, in a more random pattern. Slip a piece of cardboard under the tablecloth to protect your work surface. Peel off the backing paper and iron the motifs in place.

7 To make matching napkins, appliqué single motifs to the corners, using fusible bonding web and antifraying solution if necessary, as before.

APPLIQUÉ BED LINEN

Customized bed linen is very simple to make and will give a real lift to bedroom decor. These designs can be added along borders or scattered across the main fabric—it all depends on how adventurous you feel. The duvet cover uses a variation on the technique of cutwork appliqué, meaning that the design is cut out from the main fabric and a contrasting color is stitched underneath.

1 Draw star shapes on paper or thin cardboard and cut out. Draw around the stars on scraps of colored fabric using a fading fabric marker, leaving a ½-inch seam allowance.

2 Cut out the fabric stars, snipping into the seam allowance up to the drawn outline as shown. Do not cut into the actual star shape.

3 With wrong sides facing, iron the seam allowance back onto the star to make neat edges.

MATERIALS AND EQUIPMENT YOU WILL NEED
PENCIL • PAPER OR THIN CARDBOARD • PAPER SCISSORS • SCRAPS OF COTTON FABRIC • FADING FABRIC MARKER • DRESSMAKER'S SCISSORS • IRON • COTTON PILLOWCASE • DRESSMAKER'S PINS • NEEDLE • BASTING THREAD • SEWING MACHINE • CONTRASTING SEWING THREADS • DUVET COVER • EMBROIDERY SCISSORS

4 Position the stars along one edge of the pillowcase, pin and baste in place.

6 For the duvet cover, for each circular motif, you will need to cut out two circles of fabric in contrasting colors.

8 Use sharp embroidery scissors to cut out the star ¼ inch in from the outline, leaving the circle intact. Snip into the seam allowances as before and, with the wrong sides facing, iron the seam allowance to form a neat edge.

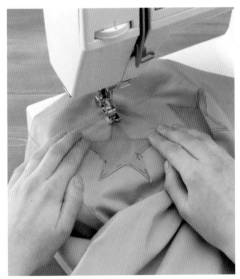

5 In a contrasting color, use a running stitch to machine-stitch the stars in place. Remove the basting threads.

7 Using the star template from the pillowcase, draw around the star on the wrong side of one of the fabric circles.

9 Place the circle with the cutout motif on top of the right side of the remaining circle, pin and baste in place. ▶

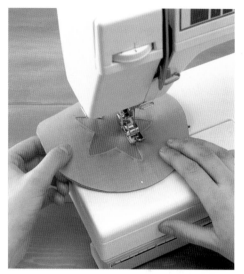

10 Machine-stitch around the edges of the star shapes and remove the basting threads.

12 Position the shapes on the duvet cover, pin and baste in place. Machine-stitch around the circles using plain and decorative stitches in contrasting colors. Remove the basting stitches.

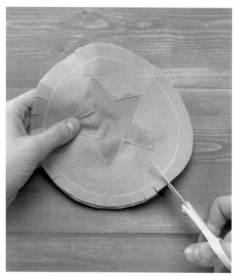

11 Snip around the circle, ½ inch in from the edge, and press in place, as before.

ORGANZA EVENING BAG

THIS EXQUISITE LITTLE BAG IS DECORATED WITH DELICATE ORGANZA FLOWERS, SIMPLY MADE OF FRINGED AND GATHERED BIAS STRIPS. A SINGLE FLOWER IS STITCHED TO THE GOLD RIBBON TIES TO NEATEN THE ENDS. THE BAG IS TOO BEAUTIFUL TO HIDE AWAY IN A DRAWER WHEN NOT IN USE—FILL IT WITH POTPOURRI OR HERBS AND HANG IT ON A DRESSING TABLE OR BEDPOST. A LARGER BAG COULD BE MADE TO HOLD A NIGHTGOWN.

1 Draw an oval shape on paper, 5½ inches long and 4½ inches at the widest point. Cut out, pin onto cream organza and cut around. Cut two pieces of blue organza 7½ inches wide and 7¾ inches high.

2 Place the two pieces of blue organza together, fold in half and machine-stitch the short side. With the right sides facing, baste to the cream organza oval, then stitch. Turn the bag right side out.

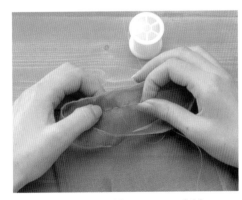

3 To make the ribbon casing, fold over ½ inch on the open edge and slip-stitch. Use transparent thread for all the hand-stitching.

4 Cut 11 different-colored organza strips on the bias, varying the width between ½ inch and 1½ inches. ▶

MATERIALS AND EQUIPMENT YOU WILL NEED

PAPER • PENCIL • TAPE MEASURE OR RULER • PAPER SCISSORS • DRESSMAKER'S PINS • CREAM ORGANZA • DRESSMAKER'S SCISSORS • 16-INCH SQUARE BLUE ORGANZA • SEWING MACHINE AND MATCHING THREADS • NEEDLE • BASTING THREAD • TRANSPARENT SEWING THREAD • SCRAPS OF CONTRASTING ORGANZA • SAFETY PIN • 20 INCHES NARROW GOLD RIBBON

5 Fringe one side of each strip by pulling and rubbing the threads. Work a line of large running stitches along the other edge of each strip.

7 Stitch each flower at the base to secure the shape.

9 Stitch the double flowers onto the bag, arranging them in a bouquet.

6 Pull the end of the thread to gather the organza, at the same time twisting the strip around your finger to create a flower shape.

8 To make a fuller flower, place two flower shapes together, one inside another. Stitch together with small stitches at the base. Make another four flowers in the same way, mixing the colors. Leave one flower single.

10 Fasten a safety pin to the end of the ribbon and thread it through the casing. Knot the ends, then stitch the single flower to the knot.

ANGELIC ONESIE

THIS ENCHANTING OUTFIT IS GUARANTEED TO MAKE ANY BABY LOOK SWEET AND GOOD! POSITION THE WINGS ON THE UPPER PART OF THE ONESIE, APPROXIMATELY WHERE THE BABY'S SHOULDER BLADES WILL LIE. THE WINGS ARE LIGHTLY PADDED WITH A LAYER OF BATTING TO GIVE A SLIGHTLY QUILTED EFFECT WHEN YOU MACHINE-STITCH THE OUTLINES. THE SAME TECHNIQUE AND DESIGN COULD BE USED TO DECORATE OTHER BABY CLOTHES.

1 Trace the wing shapes from the back of the book and make templates (see Basic Techniques). Using a fading fabric marker, draw around the top wing shape on a piece of interfacing, then iron onto the reverse of the blue fabric. Iron interfacing onto the reverse of the pink fabric.

2 Draw around the bottom wing shape on the interfacing side of the pink fabric. Cut out both shapes, leaving extra blue fabric on the edge marked "A," as shown. Repeat steps 1 and 2 for the other wing.

3 Baste the two parts of each wing together, making sure that the two pieces of interfacing butt together. ▶

MATERIALS AND EQUIPMENT YOU WILL NEED

TRACING PAPER • SOFT PENCIL • PAPER OR THIN CARDBOARD • PAPER SCISSORS • FADING FABRIC MARKER • LIGHTWEIGHT IRON-ON INTERFACING •
IRON • BLUE AND PINK JERSEY FABRIC • EMBROIDERY SCISSORS • NEEDLE • BASTING THREAD • LIGHTWEIGHT BATTING •
SEWING MACHINE AND MATCHING THREADS • ONESIE

4 Baste each wing onto a piece of batting.

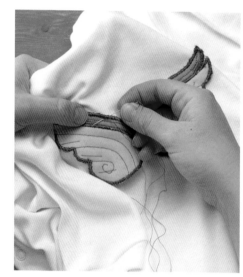

6 Position the wings on the onesie and baste in place. Slip-stitch in place, using matching threads.

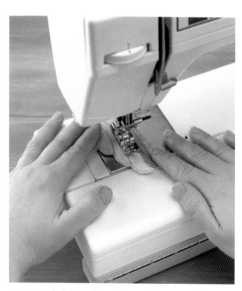

5 With blue thread, machine-stitch around the edges of the wings, using a straight stitch. Cut away the excess batting. Machine-stitch the decorative outlines. Set the machine to satin stitch and stitch around the edges of the wing.

RIBBON CUSHION

COLLECT DIFFERENT WOVEN AND BROCADE RIBBONS FOR THIS PRETTY CUSHION, THEN MACHINE-STITCH THEM ONTO A TICKING BACKGROUND, USING THE STRIPES AS A GUIDE. ALWAYS STITCH FROM THE TOP DOWN TO AVOID PUCKERING THE RIBBONS. COMPLETE THE PERIOD EFFECT WITH AN ELABORATE BRAID BORDER. IF YOU HAVE ONLY SHORT LENGTHS OF RIBBON, MAKE A SMALL PILLOW OR HERB BAG AND FILL IT WITH POTPOURRI OR LAVENDER.

1 Cut the ribbons into 14-inch lengths. Arrange them to make a pleasing design.

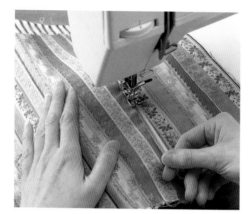

3 Add the narrow ribbons, stitching them on top of the previous layer.

5 Stitch a narrow double hem along one edge of each 13-inch square of fabric for the back opening. With the right sides facing, pin one side to each short edge of the ribbon appliqué so that the trimmed edges face inward. Stitch all around, leaving a ½-inch seam. Turn the cushion cover right side out.

2 Starting from the right-hand side, machine-stitch the wide ribbons onto the ticking background with a close zigzag stitch. Follow the stripes to keep the ribbons straight.

4 Measure the finished size of 13 x 21 inches and mark with a fading fabric marker. If necessary, trim the ribbons to this size.

6 Starting at one corner, stitch the braid all around the cushion, using a slip-stitch. Gather the braid slightly at the corners. Conceal the seam in the ends at the final corner. Insert the cushion pad.

MATERIALS AND EQUIPMENT YOU WILL NEED

EMBROIDERY SCISSORS • APPROXIMATELY 1 YARD EACH OF TEN RIBBONS, IN DIFFERENT WIDTHS • TWO 14 x 18-INCH PIECES OF TICKING, WITH THE STRIPES PARALLEL TO THE SHORT SIDES • SEWING MACHINE AND MATCHING THREADS • RULER • FADING FABRIC MARKER • TWO 13-INCH SQUARES OF FABRIC, FOR THE BACK • 61 INCHES DECORATIVE BRAID • 12 x 16-INCH CUSHION PAD

ROSE PETAL LAMPSHADE

ORGANZA WORKS PARTICULARLY WELL WHEN USED TO DECORATE A PLAIN LAMPSHADE, WITH THE LIGHT INTENSIFYING THE DELICATE COLORS. THE PETAL SHAPES ARE APPLIED IN LAYERS TO CREATE A THREE-DIMENSIONAL EFFECT.

ADJUST THE NUMBER OF PETALS, DEPENDING ON THE SIZE OF THE SHADE. MIX COLORS OF THE SAME TONE—SAY, REDS AND PINKS OR PURPLES AND LILACS. USE A LOW WATTAGE BULB AND DO NOT LEAVE THE LAMP UNATTENDED.

1 Draw two petal shapes on paper, one larger than the other. Using the large template, cut out approximately 20 petals in different shades of organza.

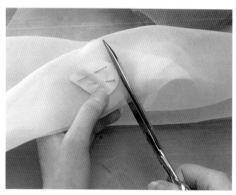

2 Cut out approximately 20 small petals, using the smaller template.

3 Using a paintbrush, glue a row of large petals 2 inches above the bottom edge of the shade, alternating the colors. Apply the glue only at the pointed end of each petal. Overlap the petals, as shown, to cover the shade.

4 Gradually work up the shade to the top, mixing large and small petals and varying the colors. Let dry.

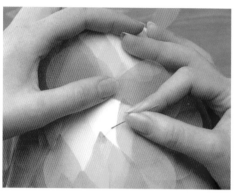

5 Alternatively, stitch each petal in place, using transparent thread. Try not to stitch through the whole shade but only into the silk or cotton surface.

6 Using a small amount of glue or a needle and transparent thread, attach the trimming around the top of the shade. Fold to the inside and glue or stitch in place.

MATERIALS AND EQUIPMENT YOU WILL NEED
PENCIL • PAPER • PAPER SCISSORS • DRESSMAKER'S PINS • 16 x 16 INCHES EACH OF THREE HARMONIOUS SHADES OF SILK ORGANZA •
DRESSMAKER'S SCISSORS • SMALL PAINTBRUSH • WHITE GLUE • SAUCER • SILK OR COTTON LAMPSHADE • NEEDLE • TRANSPARENT SEWING
THREAD • LAMPSHADE TRIMMING

LACE CUSHION

NATURAL LINEN FABRIC AND SCRAPS OF HEAVY WHITE LACE COMBINE BEAU-TIFULLY IN THIS SMALL CUSHION, FINISHED WITH PEARL BEADS AND A FRINGED EDGE. USE SEVERAL DIFFERENT STYLES OF GUIPURE LACE TO MAKE THE DESIGN INTERESTING. THE SAME IDEA WOULD WORK EQUALLY WELL ON A DRESS-ING GOWN OR DRAWSTRING BAG. TO PREVENT THE EDGES OF THE LACE MOTIFS FROM FRAYING, PAINT WITH AN ANTIFRAYING SOLUTION.

1 Draw a large letter, about 4¾ inches high, on paper and cut out to make a template. Draw around the template on the right side of one linen square. Cut out lace motifs, choosing shapes that will fit the shape of the letter.

2 Treat the lace edges with antifraying solution. Let dry. Transfer the lace motifs to the linen and baste in place.

3 Using white sewing thread, stitch the motifs in place with small stab stitches. With the wrong sides facing, hand- or machine-stitch the two squares of linen together, 1½ inches from the edge, leaving a 2-inch gap along one side. Pull away threads to make a ¾-inch fringe around the edges. Fill with a small amount of batting. Slip-stitch the gap.

4 Stitch the narrow lace edging along the stitch line to cover the stitches and decorate the edges.

5 Using a beading needle, stitch tiny pearl beads to the center of the flower-shaped lace motifs. Stitch a daisy motif to each corner of the cushion.

MATERIALS AND EQUIPMENT YOU WILL NEED

PENCIL • PAPER • PAPER SCISSORS • FADING FABRIC MARKER • TWO 8½-INCH SQUARES OF HEAVYWEIGHT NATURAL-COLORED LINEN • EMBROIDERY SCISSORS • SCRAPS OF WHITE GUIPURE LACE, INCLUDING SCROLL AND FLOWER MOTIFS • ANTIFRAYING SOLUTION • PAINTBRUSH • NEEDLE • BASTING THREAD • SEWING MACHINE (OPTIONAL) • WHITE SEWING THREAD • BATTING • 35½ INCHES NARROW WHITE LACE EDGING • BEADING NEEDLE • TINY PEARL BEADS

FELTED APPLIQUÉ ORGANZA

IN THIS BEAUTIFUL TRANSLUCENT PIECE, THE DESIGN IS MADE USING WOOL FIBERS, WHICH ARE SANDWICHED BETWEEN LAYERS OF PLASTIC NET AND ORGANZA AND THEN FELTED TOGETHER. FELTING IS QUITE A MESSY PROCESS, SO MAKE SURE YOU HAVE PLENTY OF SPACE TO WORK IN. USE AS A CURTAIN OR ROOM DIVIDER.

1 Cut the lengths of organza and plastic net in half. Place one piece of organza on top of one piece of net.

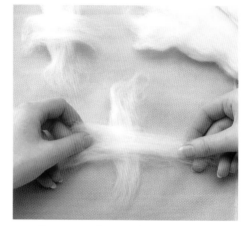

3 Place more layers of wool horizontally on top. Then place a third layer vertically on top. If desired, add silk fiber to the wool fiber.

4 Trim the edges of each mound of wool, shaping them into squares or rectangles.

2 Pull out a thin layer of wool fiber approximately 2 inches long. Lay the wool vertically on the organza, as shown. Repeat to make a design.

5 Repeat the vertical and horizontal layering process all around the edges of the organza to create a wool border, as shown.

MATERIALS AND EQUIPMENT YOU WILL NEED

DRESSMAKER'S SCISSORS • 3½ YARDS WHITE SILK ORGANZA • 3½ YARDS PLASTIC NET • 2 POUNDS WHITE MERINO WOOL FIBER • 1 OUNCE SILK FIBER (OPTIONAL) • NEEDLE AND MATCHING THREAD • LARGE PLASTIC SHEET • DISHWASHING LIQUID • IRON

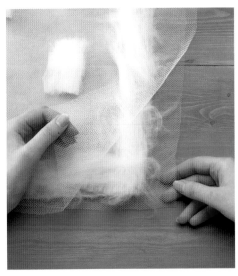

6 Place the other pieces of net on top of the design.

7 Hand-stitch the two pieces of net and organza together all around the edge with large stitches.

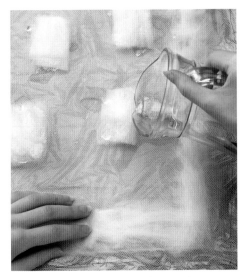

8 Protect the work surface with a sheet of plastic, then wet the fabric "sandwich" with water.

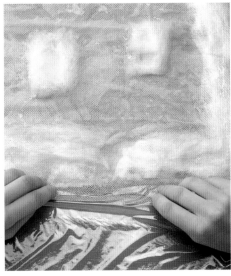

9 Apply dishwashing liquid over the fabric to help the felting process.

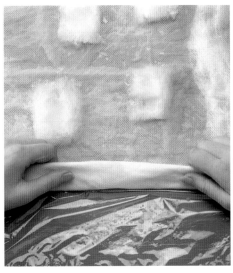

10 Roll up the fabric along one edge. Start to felt it by rubbing the surface gently with your hands in a circular movement for a few minutes, then unroll the fabric.

11 Continue rolling and felting each side for approximately 15 minutes. Wash the fabric thoroughly with warm water, open flat and let dry. ▶

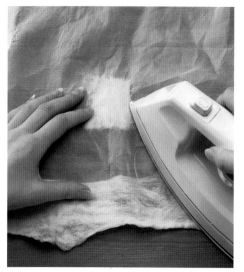

12 Remove the top layer of net and iron the felted fabric carefully.

14 The loops may be used to hang the fabric from a wooden frame to make a screen or to hang from a window or corner of a room.

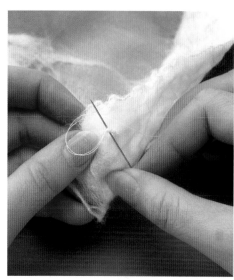

13 Stitch loops of thread onto each corner.

SEASIDE CHAIR

TRANSFORM A PLAIN DIRECTOR'S CHAIR WITH A BOLD DESIGN OF MULTICOLORED FLAGS FLYING FROM YELLOW SANDCASTLES. THE REPEATING MOTIFS ARE FUSED ONTO THE REMOVABLE CHAIR BACK WITH IRON-ON BONDING WEB, THEN MACHINE-STITCHED IN PLACE. HAND-EMBROIDERED FRENCH KNOTS ADD AN EXTRA JAUNTY FLOURISH. FIGURE OUT HOW MANY SANDCASTLES WILL FIT ON THE CHAIR BACK AND SPACE THEM EVENLY.

1 Iron the fusible bonding web onto the reverse side of the yellow fabric and of the fabrics for the flags.

3 Remove the back from the chair. Peel off the backing paper from each shape and position on the right side of the chair back, as shown, with a flag above each sandcastle turret. Iron in place.

5 Stitch a star on each sandcastle. Using embroidery floss, work a French knot at the top of each flag.

2 Draw the sandcastle and flag shapes on paper or thin cardboard to make templates and cut out (see Basic Techniques). Using a soft pencil, draw around the templates on the bonding web. Cut out.

4 Machine-stitch around the edge of each shape with a close zigzag stitch. For the flagpoles, stitch a line of straight stitch to join the flags to the turrets.

6 Cut a piece of fabric to cover the appliqué design, allowing an extra ¼-inch seam. Turn under the seam and pin in place over the back of the appliqué, with the wrong sides together. Slip-stitch in place.

MATERIALS AND EQUIPMENT YOU WILL NEED

IRON • IRON-ON FUSIBLE BONDING WEB • YELLOW FABRIC, FOR THE SANDCASTLES • SCRAPS OF DIFFERENT-COLORED FABRICS, FOR THE FLAGS • TRACING PAPER • SOFT PENCIL • PAPER OR THIN CARDBOARD • PAPER SCISSORS • DRESSMAKER'S SCISSORS • DIRECTOR'S CHAIR • IRON • SEWING MACHINE AND MATCHING THREADS • NEEDLE • SOFT COTTON EMBROIDERY FLOSS • CONTRASTING FABRIC, TO LINE THE CHAIR BACK • DRESSMAKER'S PINS

TEMPLATES

ANGELIC ONESIE PP. 79–81

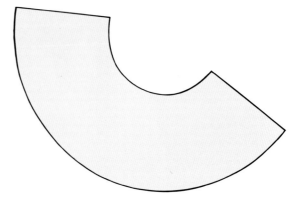

COUNTRY CANDLE SHADES PP. 48–49

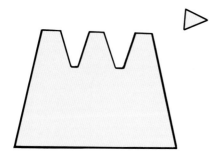

SEASIDE CHAIR PP. 92–93

ALPHABET APRON PP. 32–33

KITCHEN COLLAGE PP. 28–31

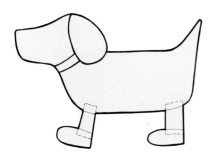

TOY BAG PP. 40–41

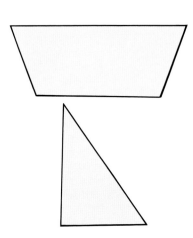

INLAID BOAT CUSHION PP. 53–55

ANGEL STOCKING PP. 37–39

HEARTS AND STARS BLANKET PP. 42–45

SUPPLIERS & ACKNOWLEDGMENTS

CONTRIBUTORS

The author and publishers would like to thank the following for their designs:

Victoria Brown
Christmas Tree Stars, Felt Curtain and Angelic Onesie.

Lucinda Ganderton
Hands and Hearts Throw, Country Candle Shades, Broderie Perse Tablecloth, Ribbon Cushion and Lace Cushion.

Jo Gordon
Heartwarming Hats.

Isabel Stanley
Mosaic Velvet Cushion.

Daniella Zimmerman Organza Evening Bag, Rose Petal Lampshade and Felted Appliqué Organza.

SUPPLIERS

Baltazor's
3262 Severn Ave.
Metairie, LA 70002
(504) 889-0333

Kreinik Manufacturing Company
3106 Timanus Lane, Suite 101
Baltimore, MD 21244
(800) 624-1928

Nancy's Notions
P.O. Box 683
Beaver Dam, WI 53916
(414) 887-0391

S & S Arts & Crafts
P.O. Box 513
Colchester, CT 06415
(800) 243-9232

INDEX

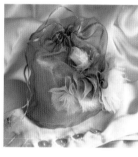